TINY
HOUSES

TINY HOUSES

Mimi Zeiger

RIZZOLI
NEW YORK

First published in the United States of America in 2009 by
RIZZOLI INTERNATIONAL PUBLICATIONS, INC.
300 Park Avenue South
New York, NY 10010
www.rizzoliusa.com

ISBN-13: 978-0-8478-3203-3
Library of Congress Control Number: 2008938981

© 2009 Rizzoli International Publications, Inc.
Texts © 2009 Mimi Zeiger

Distributed to the U.S. trade by Random House, New York

Designed by over,under

Printed and bound in China

2009 2010 2011 2012 2013/ 10 9 8 7 6 5 4 3 2 1

CONTENTS

Introduction **Mimi Zeiger** 6
BILD Design **Lowerline Residence/Domestic Shed** 11
Zero Plus Architects **Snee-Oosh Cabin** 17
UNI Architects **XS House** 23
Ronan and Erwan Bouroullec **The Floating House (La Maison Flottante)** 29
noroof architects **Slot House** 37
Olson Sundberg Kundig Allen Architects **Delta Shelter** 41
Korteknie Stuhlmacher Architecten **Parasite Las Palmas** 47
Steven Holl Architects **Turbulence House** 53
Tezuka Architects **Engawa House** 57
Bauart Architekten (for WeberHaus) **Option House** 61
BAK Arquitectos **Casa Mar Azul** 67
Counson Architectes **POB 62** 73
Atelier Tekuto **Lucky Drops** 79
Scape Architects **Front To Back House** 85
sculpt(IT) **sculpt(IT) Headquarters** 91
Gerold Peham and hobby a. **Nomad Home** 95
Michael Jantzen **M-House** 101
Todd Saunders **Blue Sky Mod Prototype Cabin** 105
Neeson Murcutt Architects **Box House** 109
Alchemy Architects **Arado Weehouse** 113
Travis Price and Spirit of Place–Spirit of Design **Floating Eco Lodge** 117
Eva Prats and Ricardo Flores with Frank Stahl **The House in A Suitcase** 121
Robbrecht en Daem **Woodland Cabine** 127
Sustain Design Studio **miniHome Solo** 131
FNP Architeckten **S(ch)austall** 137
Recetas Urbanas **Puzzle House** 143
Ivan Kroupa Architects **Snowboarders Cottage** 147
Sami Rintala, Dagur Eggertson, John Roger Holte, and Julian Fors **Boxhome** 153
Todd Saunders and Tommie Wilhelmsen **Summer House** 161
Andreas Wenning **Between Magnolia and Pine** 165
Tumbleweed Tiny House Company **Weebee House** 171
Float architectural research and design **Watershed** 177
Nils Holger Moormann **Walden** 183
Horden Cherry Lee Architects Haack + Höpfner Architekten **Micro Compact Home** 189
Parsons/ Konstfack University/ St. Etienne School **Little Houses on the Black River** 193
Marcel Krings and Sebastian Mühlhäuser **Casulo** 199

LIST OF ARCHITECTS 204

Growing up in Berkeley, the mantra "Reduce, reuse, recycle" was on every grade-schooler's lips. Recycling newspapers and soda cans, sorting glass from aluminum, we were doing our part for Mother Earth. A few years later, experiments in green living—composting (short lived), reusing plastic bags (on and off), thrifting (I have an eye for vintage)—were part and parcel of my undergrad experience. And now, on Saturdays I walk my string bag over to the Fort Greene farmers' market in Brooklyn to buy local, organic milk and produce. Occasionally I bring along salvaged plastic bags.

I am no sustainability saint. I reuse, I recycle, but what about reduce?

The 3-R slogan was set up to contend with waste management, to tackle overflowing landfills and barges of trash. As environmentally friendly language gets more sophisticated—carbon footprint, sustainable design, low impact—the first two Rs easily roll off the tongue and into practice. Which leaves "reduce."

What is that other phrase? Less is more? It seems that given an economy that runs on consumption, even the consumption of green products, there is a general feeling that it is miserly and judgmental, somehow against the American Dream, to reduce how much we take in and how much space we take up. According to the National Association of Home Builders, the average home size in the United States was 2,330 square feet in 2004, up from 1,400 square feet in 1970. That's a difference of nearly 1,000 square feet. Every one of the tiny houses featured in this book fits within that difference; these designs represent a concerted effort, often laced with critique, to live with less but to get more out of the experience. McMansion-style suburban sprawl weighs heavily on the environment, taxing already depleted resources. The recent subprime mortgage crisis revealed the dark side of three bedrooms and a two-car garage. A May 2008 report written by economist Joseph Cortright and issued by the group CEOs for Cities suggests that fuel prices and lengthy commutes popped the housing bubble. "Although housing prices are in decline almost everywhere, price declines are generally far more severe in far-flung suburbs and in metropolitan areas with weak close-in neighborhoods. The reason for this shift is rooted in the dramatic increase in gas prices over the past five years. Housing in cities and neighborhoods that require lengthy commutes and provide few transportation alternatives to the private vehicle are falling in value more precipitously than in more central, compact, and accessible places." The eco-footprint of living large goes well beyond the walls of a single house in a single development. It leaves Sasquatch-sized tracks all over. In reaction to super-sizing, groups formed to advocate scaling back, such as the Small House Society, founded in 2002 by Jay Shafer, Shay Salomon, Nigel Valdez, and Gregory Paul Johnson. Shafer's Tumbleweed Tiny House Company produces the 102-square-foot Weebee House, which is included in this collection. The society lists healthier, more cost-effective living and a better environment among the movement's benefits. People who live tiny have fewer possessions and lower utility bills, and construction of these homes requires fewer building materials and less land, so they are more efficient and sustainable.

Although data in "Shrinking the Carbon Footprint of Metropolitan America," issued by the Brooking Institute, report that municipalities across the United States—from Albany to Wichita—are actively reducing residential and transportation carbon emissions, many tiny house architects and owners head off the grid. Architect Erin Moore's totally recyclable studio for a nature writer, Watershed, is sensitive to its ecosystem. Located in Oregon's Willamette Valley, the 100-square-foot design incorporates features to support local wildlife. The Box House in New South Wales, Australia, by Nick Murcutt, is a modern design, but essentially a bush-land cabin made out of local materials. To live there you have to rough it. A 792-gallon tank stores rainwater for dishwashing and bathing, and the bathroom is an outdoor tub and neighbor's outhouse. The owners have plans to eventually install photovoltaic panels to power a hot water heater, small appliances, and lighting. Architect Tom Kundig's Delta Shelter sits on a hundred-year floodplain in the Methow River valley in eastern Washington State. The location posed a potential construction obstacle, so Kundig raised the structure on stilts to minimize potential flood damage. He also employed off-site prefabrication, a technique used by builders of many of the rural tiny houses, to minimize ecological impact.

On the urban side of things, cities, because of their high density, public transportation systems, and service access, are inherently green. Tiny houses that take advantage of small, previously unused pieces of the urban fabric map a forward-thinking, sustainable approach—an approach that might even seem counterintuitive if compared to old tree-hugger stereotypes. One of a new breed of architectural and environmental activist, Santiago Cirugeda uses temporary interventions to turn attention to the underutilized, vacant lots in Seville's old city. He used loopholes in that city's zoning legislation to build the Puzzle House, a dwelling/art project. By placing the house in a disused lot, he called attention to the need to densify Seville's urban core. Also included in this book is Scape Architects' Front to Back House—a renovated brick-fronted mews house in the trendy Islington neighborhood. The house responds more to London's market forces than to politics, but the result is a light-filled home that feels larger than its 648 square feet.

A mere 10 square feet, Casulo is the smallest project included here. Marcell Krings and Sebastian Mühlhäuser's compact set of furniture can be inserted into an existing apartment and is designed so that students and itinerant professionals can avoid the inevitable trip to Ikea for cheap, basically disposable beds, desks, and dressers, items weighed down by the costs of their manufacture and transportation on the environment. Finally, all the projects in this book emphasize design innovation when dealing with a tiny floor plan. The spaces are small, but not cramped. Reduced and reused, but responsive to light, air, and nature, with windows and decks making up for minimized living areas—and, in the case of Sculpt(IT), bathing areas: the bathtub is on the roof. It takes certain sacrifices to live in one of these homes—having fewer possessions or cooking over a wood stove—but the quality of the architecture isn't compromised. These designs illustrate ways to build homes that are reductive in scale, but not scope. By making a positive impact on the environment, each house dreams big.

The three-story Lowerline Residence rises out of New Orleans's Uptown neighborhood, its height and reflective metal exterior marking it as incongruous to the nearby shotgun houses and Creole cottages, but the house is rooted to its context. The upper floors periscope up to capture a view of the Mississippi River, while the lower level maintains the scale and texture of the adjacent structures. The two-family structure was finished just as Hurricane Katrina hit the city, but luckily, understanding the preexisting threat of water and damp, BILD Design had already raised it off the ground.

With two living units stacked on top of each other, the design rethinks affordable housing in New Orleans, proposing a denser building type. The apartments are modest, with off-the-shelf fixtures and cabinets, but high ceilings and river views offset the small footprints. The tall interior volumes also provide an environmentally friendly approach to cooling in a warm climate, especially when combined with ceiling fans. The ceilings are high enough to allow heat to rise and escape through upper-level transom windows. The spaces and materials—such as the galbanum exterior (a standing seam cladding that minimizes heat gain via reflection)—have a loftlike feel, a reference to the industrial architecture of New Orleans's nearby waterfront.

LOWERLINE RESIDENCE/ DOMESTIC SHED

New Orleans, Louisiana 2005

BILD Design

SQUARE METER
100 93
SQUARE FEET

SQUARE METER
80 74
SQUARE FEET

SQUARE METER
100093
SQUARE FEET

SQUARE METER
80074
SQUARE FEET

Located on the Swinomish Indian reservation, tribal vernacular architecture and the natural beauty of the site—a marine forest overlooking a bay—inspired the Snee-oosh Cabin's design. To honor the spirit of the place, Zero Plus Architects created a modern "lean-to" set on a wooden platform. The facade is almost entirely glass, which blurs distinctions between inside and outside. Fir trees surround the house, and it's the forest, not the glass skin, that gives a sense of enclosure. The architects minimized the footprint and strategically placed the structure to protect the oldest trees on the site. Sitting on eight concrete feet, the house treads lightly on the forest floor's complex topsoil layer. The floor platform hovers above the understory growth, allowing the forest to extend beneath it.

The Snee-oosh interior is uncluttered: a great room augmented by an open kitchen and efficient bedrooms. An industrial ceiling fan works with openings in the roof to create passive ventilation. A carapace-like roof shelters the living spaces—a steel exoskeleton supports a wooden ceiling and an oversized foam panel roof. Prefabricated truss and roof components eased construction and helped reduce impact on the sensitive environment.

SNEE-OOSH CABIN

Deception Pass, Washington 2007
Zero Plus Architects

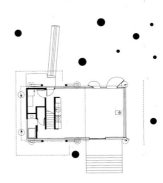

1147107

Clifton Street is a quiet residential corner of Cambridge, homey with trees and detached, single-family homes. Within this semiurban fabric UNI Architects developed four lots, each with a different-sized dwelling (XS, S, M, and L), to maximize density. As the last piece of the composition, the three-story XS House plays off its neighbors, whose close proximity presented the challenge: how to bring light into the house while maintaining privacy. The solution is three 16-by-22-foot boxes, with every level rotated slightly to create corner skylights. The interiors are flooded with natural light without excessive exposure.

In contrast to the larger homes on the site, which are clad in cedar shingles, tongue and groove planks, and steel, the XS House is finished in marine plywood. The material's pronounced grain unifies the structure's shifting shape. Inside, only the oak plywood staircase that links the floors divides the spaces. The architects used materials to create a distinct mood on each level: white marble is cool and luminous in the kitchen and dining area on the first floor, while warm, oak plywood makes for a cozy second-story living room.

XS HOUSE

Cambridge, Massachusetts 2006
UNI Architects

Located on the banks of the Seine is the Centre National de l'Estampe et de l'Art Imprimé (CNEAI), the national center of print art. The institution commissioned the Paris-based designers Ronan and Erwan Bouroullec to create a live/work houseboat for its artist-in-residence program. True to the city's poetic history, the barge docks at the impressionists' island in Chatou, best known for Renoir's painting, Luncheon of the Boating Party. Working in collaboration with architect Jean-Marie Finot and naval architect Denis Daversin, the designers constructed the floating home in Le Havre and then towed it more than 100 miles upriver.

A streamlined aluminum skin wraps the mostly open cabin space. In order to blend the 75-foot-long boat into the island landscape, the designers built a wooden terrace around the aluminum shell with the intent that creeping vines (sprouting from planters on deck) would grow into a verdant facade—a technique that keeps the interior cool. Inside, there are windows only on the Seine side (the bank side is left blank for privacy), which are nearly level with the water's edge. Light reflects off the surface, decorating the cedar walls in aqueous ripples.

THE FLOATING HOUSE (LA MAISON FLOTTANTE)

Paris, France 2006

Ronan and Erwan Bouroullec with architects
Jean-Marie Finot and Denis Daversin

Brooklyn-based architects Margarita McGrath and Scott Oliver's transformation of an over two-hundred-year-old existing row house began with a tree. Located in the dense Fort Greene neighborhood, the vinyl-sided, brick structure is set back from the street and a sixty-foot-tall maple dominates the front yard. Wanting to preserve the tree, the architects decided not to build out into the yard, a decision that left the space free to be an outside room. Instead, they cut a vertical slot in the facade to frame the tree. That move conceptually slices through the whole building—the galvanized stair rises from the basement to the second floor in that zone. Responding to the climate, the vertical slot and clerestory windows passively heat the home in the winter months; in the summer the tree canopy provides cooling shade.

The Slot House is part modern renovation and part archeological dig. When the architects began demolition for the remodel they found cedar timbers and hand-cut bricks from around 1800. The loftlike interior preserves these finds. Using off-the-shelf plywood and sheets of galvanized "lobster trap" mesh; they created an architecture that responds to the structure's quirky moments and tight conditions. The main living quarters is just 600 square feet, with a 400-square-foot rental unit at the rear of the ground floor. A second sleeping area is squeezed into the space between the kitchen cabinets. The design makes use of every possible inch, leaving open areas so that the space feels expansive.

SLOT HOUSE

Brooklyn, New York 2005
noroof architects

The Methow River valley in eastern Washington State is a hundred-year floodplain, a fact that posed a potential obstacle to the construction of the Delta Shelter, a weekend cabin located in the valley. By raising the structure on stilts, architect Tom Kundig hoped to minimize potential flood damage. To cut down on the project's ecological impact, prefabricated pieces of the steel structure were bolted together quickly on site. Large windows on each side of the 20-by-20-foot cabin take advantage of the cabin's tree-house-like vantage point, offering views of the surrounding mountains and forest. Shutters protect the weathered-steel and glass facade from weather extremes and vandalism. Four 10-by-18-foot shutters maneuver over the glass via a hand-cranked cable-and-pulley system when it's time to close the house for the season.

The cabin's functions are divvied up between two floors: two bedrooms and one and a half bathrooms on the second floor, a living room and open kitchen on the third. Continuing the industrial motif of the rusty steel exterior, plywood finishes the interior walls, ceilings, and stairs, accented by exposed steel beams and fasteners. The hand wheel used to close the shutters, installed prominently in the living room, resembles a piece of found-object art.

DELTA SHELTER

Mazama, Washington 2005
Olson Sundberg Kundig Allen Architects

Korteknie Stuhlmacher's Parasite is not your typical "green roof." The citron-colored structure perches on the roof of the elevator shaft of the Las Palmas building, the bright dwelling standing out against Rotterdam's harbor's industrial gray. Designed as part of an exhibition during the city's year as a European Capital of Culture, one of thirty prototypical proposals by an international group of architects, the house is a symbol on the skyline. It broadcasts the need for flexible, ecological, and low-cost housing. Because the Parasite is installed in a leftover, underutilized site—drawing electrical power and water service from the "host" building—it reduces the need for urban sprawl.

Solid laminated timber panels made from European waste wood construct the Parasite's walls, floors, and roof. Each prefabricated piece was precut to size and delivered to the site for quick and easy assembly. Although the parasitic form is eccentric, the two-story layout is straightforward. Core functions, like the kitchen and bath, are grouped with the stair, leaving the living and sleeping areas unobstructed. Accenting the stripped-down aesthetic, the interior panels are left untreated and uncovered, with simple windows punched into the walls.

PARASITE LAS PALMAS

Rotterdam, Netherlands 2001–5

Korteknie Stuhlmacher Architecten

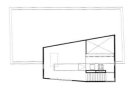

SQUARE METER

91585

SQUARE FEET

TURBULENCE HOUSE

Abiquiu, New Mexico 2005

Steven Holl Architects

An iceberg poised atop a desert mesa, the Turbulence House is perhaps a droll comment on global warming. Designed by architect Steven Holl, the hollowed-out form appears molded by the winds gusting through its center. The architect used parametric software to determine the dynamic shape and worked with sheet metal fabricator A. Zahner and Co. to transform the digital drawings into the house's aluminum shell. Thirty Galvalum (a reflective material that minimizes cooling loads) panels were prefabricated and bolted together on site. The construction process lightened the impact of construction on the sensitive desert environment.

The compact, amorphic structure supports all the comforts of home: kitchen and living areas on the ground floor and sleeping loft and study on the upper level. It is also a textbook of green construction techniques such as solar power and locally sourced and non-off gassing materials. Photovoltaic roof panels generate enough electricity to power domestic electrical loads, including the radiant floor heating system. Holl strategically placed windows to face north, which lessens heat gain on the exposed mesa. Operable slotted openings high on the facade let hot air escape, ventilating the living spaces. A cistern on the south side of the house collects storm water runoff, which is recycled to irrigate the arid site.

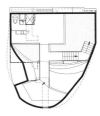

The traditional Japanese *engawa* is a covered walkway that wraps around the house. Like the vernacular veranda, it is not only a sheltered place to sit; it is also low-tech climate control, providing protection from solar gain, wind, and rain. Tezuka Architects' Engawa House is a 53-foot-long porch—a study in indoor-outdoor living. Nine glass sliding doors run the length of the narrow structure and open onto a large courtyard. Although the house is located on a tight Tokyo site, it has an expansive feel. The client shares the outdoor space with the opposite property, owned by his mother.

Essentially an elongated wooden box, the structure is simple. Two 50-foot steel beams span the long facades. This frees the interior space of any columns. To maintain privacy, clerestory windows sit high in the street-side facade. Operable, they aid in cross-ventilation, allowing warm air to escape and fresh breezes to flow inside. Defining the living and kitchen areas and separating them from the office, bedroom, and bathroom is a large shelving and closet unit. A counterpoint to the open floor plan, an oversized wood table designed by the architects sits at the center of the living area. Paired with a minimal fireplace, it is a place to gather for meals and the heart of the home.

ENGAWA HOUSE

Tokyo, Japan 2003
Tezuka Architects

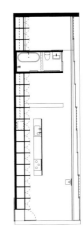

Developed by architect Peter C. Jakob of Bauart for the modular home manufacturer WeberHaus, the Option House is a cubic take on contemporary Swiss housing. The house's small footprint ensures low impact on the environment, yet WeberHaus offers "options" that grow the basic version. L- or U-shaped variations extend the floor plates, and features such as awnings and terraces are also available.

The highly functional interior feels like a shotgun house. It's a straight shot through the rectangular plan: dining room, kitchen, and living room. A stair rises to the office, bathroom, and bedroom. Four large windows, strategically placed around the two-story, wood-clad volume, flood the living spaces with natural light. Ecologically conscious, hearty insulation wraps the whole building envelope. Heated by a wood-burning stove (with electric heaters in the kitchen and the bathroom), the home's minimal design limits dependence on fossil fuels.

OPTION HOUSE

Location varies 2000
Bauart (for WeberHaus)

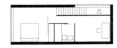

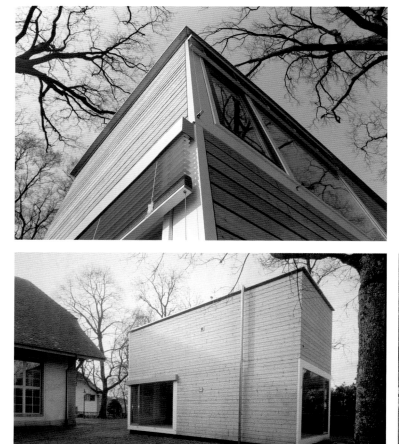

CASA MAR AZUL

Mar Azul, Argentina 2006
BAK Arquitectos

Mar Azul is a small resort town on Argentina's Atlantic coast, just south of Villa Gesell, a historically freethinking community. The area's landscape is unique: a pine forest abuts a sandy beach. Given the sensitive site, the clients wanted a house with low impact on the environment. BAK Arquitectos's design sits among forty-three pines and integrates some of the trees into the building.

Viewed from the outside, the forest is reflected in the floor-to-ceiling windows, which define the living and dining areas. The distinction between inside and outside blurs on the inside: large aluminum and glass doors slide open to the wood deck. Rough, cast-in-place concrete walls fold around the kitchen and bedrooms to create privacy. A cantilevered reinforced-concrete roof (slightly sloped to allow rainwater runoff) tops the entire structure.

The scheme is stripped to its essentials but responsive to the climate. Because the maritime forest is shady and breezy, even on hot days, the architects didn't have to insulate the concrete, which kept construction costs low. BAK Arquitectos also designed the house's minimal and ecologically responsible furniture, building the benches and table out of recycled Canadian pine recovered from shipping crates.

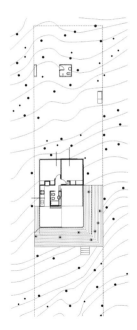

POB 62

Baraque de Fraiture, Belgium 2002

Counson Architectes

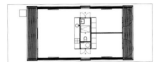

The POB 62 prototype comes with a high-tech name tag, but its profile immediately conjures up traditional notions of home, complete with wood framing and wood shingles. The front and rear elevations are iconic—rectangles topped with a peaked roof. Although sketched with a crayon-drawing simplicity, these glazed facades are fairly sophisticated. To contend with the challenge of heat gain and loss, architect Bertrand Counson extended a louvered, larch-wood shelter out from the glazed surface. The shade structure protects the house from direct summer sun and creates a porch. Providing an additional 155 square feet of living area, these two porches blur the line between inside and outside.

Counson's light-filled prototype design is a reaction to the poorly designed and cheaply built housing he saw springing up in this native Belgium. Located in Baraque de Fraiture, the POB 62 is, essentially, a model home. Potential buyers can rent it for a weekend for a test drive. The house models its efficiency: a service core containing the kitchen and bathroom bisects the rectangular floor plan. On one side of the core is the living room; two bedrooms are on the other. The minimalist interior is finished almost entirely in plywood. The surface glows with the addition of natural light, giving the otherwise minimalist home a warm feeling.

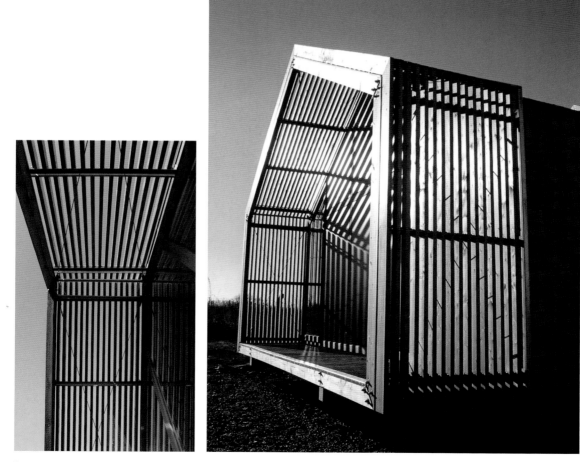

LUCKY DROPS

Tokyo, Japan 2005
Atelier Tekuto

Lucky Drops sits on a narrow plot of land not much wider than an alleyway—a thin, leftover slice of land at the end of a row of three mansard-roof townhouses. Measuring 10 feet at the street, the site shrinks to two and a half feet. A reinvention of a traditional form, the 650-square-foot home resembles a *bonbori*, a Japanese paper lantern. Fiber-reinforced plastic serves as a skin on the steel-rib structure. The translucent material lets daylight deep into the building, while at night Lucky Drops glows from within.

Skinny and 96 feet long, it was a challenge to accommodate the necessary household program. Architect Yasuhiro Yamashita placed the main living area, kitchen, and bathroom below grade. Visitors enter the ground-level foyer and face a dynamic, forced perspective of the interior (the space foreshortens), before walking down a flight of metal steps to the minimal living room. Once inside, the space seems surprisingly expansive, a trick of light and perspective. Both the first floor and the catwalklike second floor are built out of perforated steel grating to maximize light in the small, but loftlike, home.

Brick-fronted mews houses dating from the eighteenth and nineteenth centuries line the cobbled streets of London's Islington neighborhood. The structures, generally built as workers' quarters or stables, are traditionally dark and cramped, but, located in a popular district, they command top dollar. With the Front to Back House Scape architects transformed an existing mews house into a light-filled volume. Enclosed on all three sides by adjacent buildings and a schoolyard, with only two small street-facing windows, the structure lacked daylight. To illuminate the interior, the architects cut a slot in the roof. Running from front to back, the skylight aligns with a new stair. Translucent acrylic balustrade panels enclose the stair and diffuse light into the surrounding spaces.

Providing more than light and circulation, the stair also organizes both floors: at ground level its underside provides storage—tailored for the clients' bicycles, coats, and an AV system—on one side, while on the other it hides a kitchenette and guest bathroom. On the second floor the stair divides the bedroom and bathroom. A glass platform connects the two spaces. This small insertion radically reshapes the existing structure, allowing a view of the sky from deep in the house.

FRONT TO BACK HOUSE

Islington, London, United Kingdom 2007
Scape Architects

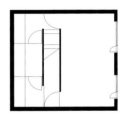

Just under 8 feet wide, sculpt(IT) founders Pieter Peerlings and Silvia Mertens's home may be skinny, but it is no shrinking violet; it revels in exhibitionism. Fitting snugly between two drab neighbors, the four-story structure is located in a former red-light district and outfitted with an entirely glass facade. Neon lights frame the each window, making the act of living into a peepshow. Every level is tinted a different color: blue, red, green, and white—at night, each glows, alluring or luridly. The transparency calls attention to every extraneous detail of the modern home. While not overtly sustainable, the house is a comment on consumption.

A decidedly simple steel frame supports the four wood floors, with program neatly and simply divided among them: the sculpt(IT) office is on the ground floor, kitchen and dining areas on the second floor, living room on the third, and the bedroom on the fourth. A tight spiral staircase connects the floors. Every function is exposed. On the sleeping level, the double bed, flush with the windows, leaves no room for privacy. The architects also designed the home's unenclosed, freestanding stainless-steel toilet. On the roof, soaking in the open-air tub is a small bit of luxury in the otherwise minimal quarters, but it is also the only place in the house for a bath.

SCULPT(IT) HEADQUARTERS

Antwerp, Belgium 2008

sculpt(IT)

Salzburg-based Gerold Peham's Nomad Home is decidedly mod—modern and modular. Streamlined, its curves echo movement, linking the concept to the nomadic lifestyle of the dwelling's potential users. Both house and product, it is not unlike a trailer. Since it is not tied to property, it can be owned, yet moved at whim to a new location. Assembled out of prefabricated modules, the Nomad Home goes up as easily as it comes down, and each section is designed to fit on the back of truck.

At the heart of the project concept is flexibility and quick adaptation to a changing global condition. The basic Nomad Home module comes equipped with a bathroom, kitchen, and bedroom, and is readily mounted on a simple foundation. Plumbing and electric feeds simply plug in, with an optional solar energy system. Features such as a larch-wood terrace and sunshade, extra rooms, or a garage are sold as accessories. The inside of the Nomad Home is clad almost entirely in linoleum panels, which, as taste in color changes, can be swapped out for more fashionable hues.

NOMAD HOME

Seekirchen, Austria 2005

Gerold Peham and hobby a.

An eccentric prefabricated home, architect Michael Jantzen's M-house arrives flat-packed. Assembled on almost any site, it resembles a monochromatic shantytown—all haphazard angles. Yet there is a rationale behind the apparent madness. Derived from Jantzen's M-vironment system, hinged rectangular panels attach to a steel structural frame set on concrete footings. The hinges account for the structure's freeform profile; solid or louvered concrete composite panels fold in or out in response to programmatic requirements. Louvered panels, positioned around the exterior decks, deflect heat and block rain.

The 65-foot-long, 36-foot-wide, 23-foot-tall M-house intermingles inside and outside spaces. The finished design of the 500-square-foot interior is up to the owner, but shaded decks, complete with built-in seating areas, extend the compact living quarters. M-house is outfitted to hook up to a standard power grid, but it can be equipped with the optional auxiliary Energy Gathering and Storage Pod, which uses photovoltaic cells or a wind turbine to generate electricity.

M-HOUSE

Location varies 2007
Michael Jantzen

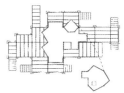

Architect Todd Saunders's proto-type cabin design for modular home manufacturers Blue Sky Mod brings environmental responsibility to the modern prefab trend. Because the cabin is designed for installation on rural sites, low environmental impact drives the scheme. This means creating a structure with a small footprint. Specifications call for local and re-cycled materials and for processes that minimize waste.

Saunders's design takes inspiration from Nordic cottages. The proto-type is clad in cedar planks and the extended roof eaves shade the facade, protecting the interior from excessive heat gain. The house's functions are separated into two small structures: the 288-square-foot dwelling cabin and the bathing cabin, which contains an ecologically friendly compost toilet, shower, and wood-burning sauna. Both pieces sit on a 43-by-16-foot cedar plank deck, making the cabin's exterior spaces livable and connected to the natural context.

BLUE SKY MOD PROTOTYPE CABIN

Location varies 2005

Todd Saunders

BOX HOUSE

New South Wales, Australia 1999
Neeson Murcutt Architects

A cube—20 feet high by 20 feet long by 20 feet wide—sited on New South Wales bush land, the shedlike Box House is a study in restraint. Yet the design, by Nick Murcutt, son of architect Glenn Murcutt, is hardly parsimonious: 1¼-inch-thick yellow stringy bark timber encloses the volume on three sides (the structural frame is local spotted gum wood), and the north facade is entirely glass. This small combination of architectural elements makes for a spacious interior with a rich materiality. The outside wood has weathered to a dusty brown-gray, while the inside is a warm, reddish hue. Life in the Box House centers on the double-height living room, but stretches out into the landscape. Folding glass doors on the ground floor open up to a deck and capture views of the sprawling hills.

The bareness of the design makes daily tasks take on a camping feel: a ladder reaches the sleeping alcove, and the kitchen is spare. To wash dishes, rainwater has to be collected from the roof and stored in a 792-gallon tank. The bathroom consists of a cauldronlike outdoor tub and a nearby outhouse. Plans are in the works for a storage shed topped with solar collectors. The photovoltaic panels will power a hot water heater, small appliances, and lighting.

33 631 SQUARE METER SQUARE FEET

The WeeHouse is a prefab housing system designed to encourage efficient living. Alchemy Architects' Geoffrey Warner's scheme is a reaction against the damage caused by suburban overbuilding. WeeHouse modules can be configured in single and double arrangements to create a variety of house styles, each with a modern aesthetic and limited environmental impact. Fabrication occurs off site in factories that reduce construction waste. At 14 feet wide, the maximum width allowed by roadway regulations, the modules are trucked to the site and installed on footings.

Located in rural western Wisconsin, the Arado WeeHouse is a study in minimal living. Essentially it is an oxidized steel–clad box, lined with fir on the interior. There is no electricity and no internal bathroom. But what the house lacks in amenities it makes up for in design and materials. Oak shelves and stainless-steel cabinets maximize storage. Tall, sliding glass doors on each long elevation frame the landscape, so the small cabin feels as big as all outdoors.

ARADO WEEHOUSE

Lake Pepin, Wisconsin 2004

Alchemy Architects

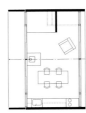

FLOATING ECO LODGE

Yarapa River, Amazon, Peru 1999

Travis Price and Spirit of Place—Spirit of Design
program, Catholic University of America

In the summer of 1999, Catholic University of America students enrolled in the Spirit of Place—Spirit of Design program traveled to the Amazon rain forest on an expedition to understand native construction and ecological biodiversity. There, they built the Floating Eco Lodge, which was commissioned by the Yacumama Lodge, an eco-friendly resort dedicated to environmental and cultural preservation located 75 miles west of Iquitos, Peru, on the banks of the Yarapa River—a tributary of the upper Amazon.

Completed on site in eight days, the lodge is constructed out of indigenous materials: an exterior iron-wood structure sits atop a balsa-wood raft, which allows it to float. The roof combines thatching (a technique of the local Yarapa Indians) and metal sheeting. The roof's unique curved shape allows daylight into the interior, but blocks direct sunlight and heat. The form also creates a thermal chimney that vents hot air. The students constructed the lodge's simple furniture: a small bench, table, and suspended bed, which swings with the river current.

Although the House in a Suitcase was inspired in part by Marcel Duchamp's arty Boîte-en-valise and in part by Louis Vuitton luggage—compact closets and steamer trunks for the jet set—it's actually designed for minimum consumption. The installation is so reductive that it buffers against accumulation. A temporary home located on the roof of a Barcelona apartment building, the project is somewhere between a hotel room and an apartment—it unpacks when occupied. A set of trunklike compartments greets visitors. The plywood boxes disassemble to reveal living spaces. The kitchen box, 6½ feet long by 5½ feet wide by 4 feet tall, hides a stainless-steel sink, a refrigerator, and countertops; a breakfast table emerges, as do the glasses cupboard and the pantry.

Like a cabinet of curiosities, the bedroom furniture (a slightly larger box than the kitchen) unpacks: the double bed slides out from under the living area platform, and the closet's doors convert to a folding screen, shielding the dressing area. Carefully detailed, the architecture makes accommodations for even the smallest of objects such as jewelry and pills.

THE HOUSE IN A SUITCASE

Barcelona, Spain 2005

Eva Prats and Ricardo Flores with Frank Stahl

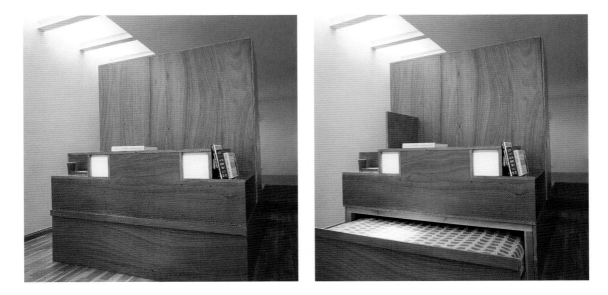

Ghent-based architects Paul Robbrecht and Hilde Daem's Woodland Cabine sits at the bank of a small creek in a Belgian forest. The location lends itself to fairy-tale fantasy. The architects' design takes its cues from log cabin construction, and a bit of Smurf village architecture. The walls trace the outline of two intersecting circles, which produces an organic form. The roof, a flat plane floating on top, collects leaves, mirroring the surrounding forest floor and blending the little building into the landscape.

The Woodland Cabine's Spartan interior space, interrupted only by a wood-burning stove, contains just enough room for a sleeping area and a seating area. (Cooking and bathing functions take place outside.) Yet the construction technique employed gives the structure a material richness and texture. Stacked pieces of square-section lumber form the walls. The short lengths interlock, shifting along the cabin's circumference. Underscoring the hutlike interior, the walls not only curve, but taper inward. A floor-to-ceiling glass door and adjoining window that looks out over the water give perspective to the intimate quarters.

WOODLAND CABINE

South of Flanders, Belgium 2001
Robbrecht en Daem

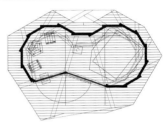

The Canadian-designed miniHome Solo updates the trailer home with modern aesthetics and an ecological sensibility. Sustainable materials are used to construct a clean, loftlike form. Built on a permanent steel frame, with three axles and wheels, the prefabricated home is classified as a travel-trailer, a design feature perfect for living off the grid. Towable to any location, rural or urban, it's equipped with a detachable hitch, electric brakes, and running lights.

Once installed, the miniHome is a model of energy efficiency; its small size and good insulation combine with passive heating and cooling techniques to reduce electrical loading. The house layout features well-placed operable windows to maximize light, air circulation and ventilation, and solar gains in the winter. Solar panels installed on an aluminum canopy over the front door produce enough energy to run lighting and high-efficiency appliances. For an extra boost, the Sustain Design Studio offers an optional 400-watt wind turbine that mounts on a 16-foot-tall mast. According to the designers, miniHome uses one hundredth of the electrical energy of a 2,000-square-foot conventional home. A patch of "green roof" on the miniHome's exterior is not large enough to have significant environmental impact, but it is a symbol of the design's ecological good will.

MINIHOME SOLO

Location varies 2006
Sustain Design Studio

German wordplay is at the heart of FNP Architeckten's project: an existing pig stable, converted into a showroom. The original building was damaged in World War II and patched over the years. Zoning and site restraints, along with a tight budget, made a new, ground-up structure impossible. More than a standard remodel, the architects left the eighteenth-century stone stable untouched, inserting a timber-frame structure inside the crumbling shell—a house within a house.

Or, in this case, a *s(ch)austall*. Warm and inviting, the plywood interior mirrors the masonry facade, with a gap between the new and old construction. The walls and openings mimic the ruin's eccentric details. A squat, floor-level window frames the former pig entrance, a sly gesture to the structure's pigsty history.

S(CH)AUSTALL

Pfalz, Germany 2004
FNP Architeckten

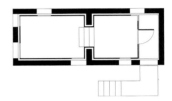

Recetas Urbanas, the name of Santiago Cirugeda's Seville-based practice, translates as "urban prescriptions." The Puzzle House is one of the firm's strategic remedies—a temporary intervention that calls attention to the underutilized, vacant lots in Seville's old city. Installed for a month in the Plaza de la Mina of Cadiz in a recycled lot, the small house is both an idea for living small and an art project. Loopholes in the city's zoning legislation allowed for its construction.

To outwit municipal ordinances, the prefabricated structure was treated as a "moveable good." This allowed temporary installation as an art piece. Bright yellow legs lift the cubic house to the same height as an existing wall, and highlight its objectlike design. Lightweight panels on a metal frame clad the house. With handrail details that recall construction site barriers or police barricades, the small yellow balcony overlooks the street. When the Puzzle House was installed in Seville, a band performed from the perch—a loud, public spectacle broadcasting the reclaimed space.

PUZZLE HOUSE

Seville, Spain 2003
Recetas Urbanas

SNOWBOARDERS COTTAGE

Herlíkovice, Czech Republic 2001
Ivan Kroupa Architects

Sited at the edge of a national park—conveniently at the foot of a ski run—the Snowboarders Cottage is a wry update on the traditional Czech cabin. Although the original family cabin had fallen into disrepair, architect Ivan Kroupa wanted to maintain the traditional connection to the landscape and sensitivity to natural materials in the new structure. Small and sitting lightly on the earth, the simple form responds to the mountainous environment.

The downhill, north facade is clad in treated spruce planks and faces the cableway station, which lifts skiers and snowboarders up to the top of the run. Left blank for privacy, the facade buffers the cabin against mountain winds and storms. Facing uphill, large windows cut into the titanium-zinc southern side allow viewers to look out over a terrace. The deck, which at 138 square feet is bigger than the main floor, extends the house's livable area in both the summer and the winter. Inside, clad completely in spruce planks, the home is compact and shiplike. The two-story space centers around the hearth: a built-in seating area made of finished plywood wraps the fireplace. Adjacent to the kitchen, the nook provides a spot to warm up and dry out after hitting the slopes.

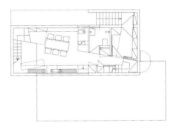

Designed by a team of architects and artists, Boxhome is a response to Scandinavia's McMansion boom. Long Nordic winters mean that large houses have to be climate controlled for more than half the year, a huge drain on energy resources. By limiting the conditioned area, this petite prototype, just 63 square feet, is both economical and ecological. When oriented south, so that the window in the 18-foot wide facade gets full sun exposure, the structure can absorb and retain enough solar radiation to not need additional winter heating.

The space is tight, but all the basic living functions are covered in four small rooms: kitchen and dining area, bathroom, living room, and bedroom. To make the compact home livable, the team paid careful attention to the quality of the spaces. Natural light spills in from windows set high in the aluminum facade and illuminates the different types of wood used in the interior spaces: cypress, birch, spruce, and red oak. The material's irregular textures and natural scent combine to create a warm, cozy environment—a retreat from Oslo's chilly clime.

BOXHOME

Oslo, Norway 2007

Sami Rintala, Dagur Eggertson, John Roger Holte, and Julian Fors

Perched on the edge of one of Norway's most dramatic fjords, 260 feet above sea level, the Summer House fits into its natural surroundings but still is a distinct form. Thirty yards away, 100-foot-high waterfalls pour into a forest stream. Visitors use an old stone footbridge to cross over the stream to reach the remote retreat. Once at the site, the views are vast, almost hypnotic.

The architects separated the retreat's functions into separate cabins: one is for sleeping and eating; the other, when completed, will house the study and bathroom. With a curved back wall and glazed front facade, the 160-square-foot wood-framed cabin (insulated with recycled newspapers) scoops up the view. The architects incorporated relaxed, outdoor living into the design, since the cabin is used in the summer, when daylight lasts for nearly twenty hours. A long, narrow wood deck extends from the sled-shaped cabin and wraps around existing trees. Not only does it provide a viewing platform, it more than doubles the home's livable space.

SUMMER HOUSE

Hardanger Fjord, Norway 2003

Todd Saunders and Tommie Wilhelmsen

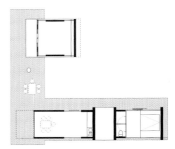

Architect Andreas Wenning's *baumraum* (tree house), Between Magnolia and Pine, transforms the pleasure of a childhood escape into a modern living space. Located in two trees in a private garden near Osnabrück, Germany, the tree house with elevated terrace is an escape from the ground plane and a relaxing retreat.

Steel frames lift the treehouse 13 feet into the leafy canopy. Ecologically responsible, screws and nails never puncture the trunks, preserving the trees' health. A stair leads to a large terrace landing equipped with an outdoor shower. Clad in tatajuba boards and insulated by environmentally friendly rock wool insulation, the wood-framed tree house sits three feet higher. Inside, wide oak benches with storage drawers wrap three walls. Topped with cushions, they double as both sleeping and lounging spots. Although the cozy space is equipped with a stereo system and artificial lighting, it always maintains a connection to nature. Corner ribbon windows frame the pines, while a large picture window offers a cinematic panorama of the nearby valley.

BETWEEN MAGNOLIA AND PINE

Osnabrück, Germany 2007

Andreas Wenning

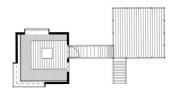

The Weebee House is just one of a number of petite abodes offered by the Tumbleweed Tiny House Company. Founded by Jay Shafer, the company sells both assembled houses (towed to site on a trailer axle) and floor plans for self-construction. Shafer's venture promotes an ethos of low environmental impact, energy efficiency, and luxury in simple living. Five of the company's eight styles are around 100 square feet, and Shafer lives in a 96-square-foot home of his own design. Each house's plan strips out wasted or unused space such as hallways and stairwells, and maximizes storage where possible.

The Weebee's pine-finished interior fits a living area, desk, small kitchen (complete with stainless-steel appliances and counters), and wet bath into its minimal footprint. To reach the queen-sized sleeping loft tucked under the pitched roof, occupants use a built-in ladder. The house comes equipped with a propane boat heater and is wired to plug into an outside electricity source, but with simple conversions it can adapt to a solar-powered system.

WEEBEE HOUSE

Location varies 2007

Tumbleweed Tiny House Company

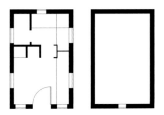

A studio for a nature writer, Watershed sits on a small piece of land along the Mary's River adjacent to riparian wetlands, which are part of a project to restore hydrological and ecological function to the area. Architect Erin Moore's design is a poetic response to the sensitive environment—the owner's one criterion was to hear rain pitter-patter against the roof canopy. Since the site has no road access or electricity, pieces of the structure were prefabricated and assembled in place: a cedar-clad steel frame supported by simple concrete foundation piers. To ensure no long-term damage to the ecosystem, the shed can be easily decamped and recycled.

Architectural details reveal the landscape's abundant wildlife: birds, deer, and other animals gather around the water collection basin at the front of the shed. Tunnels under the studio serve as small homes for reptiles and amphibians, viewable through a floor-level window.

WATERSHED

Willamette Valley, Oregon 2007
Float architectural research and design

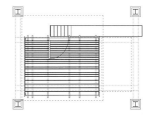

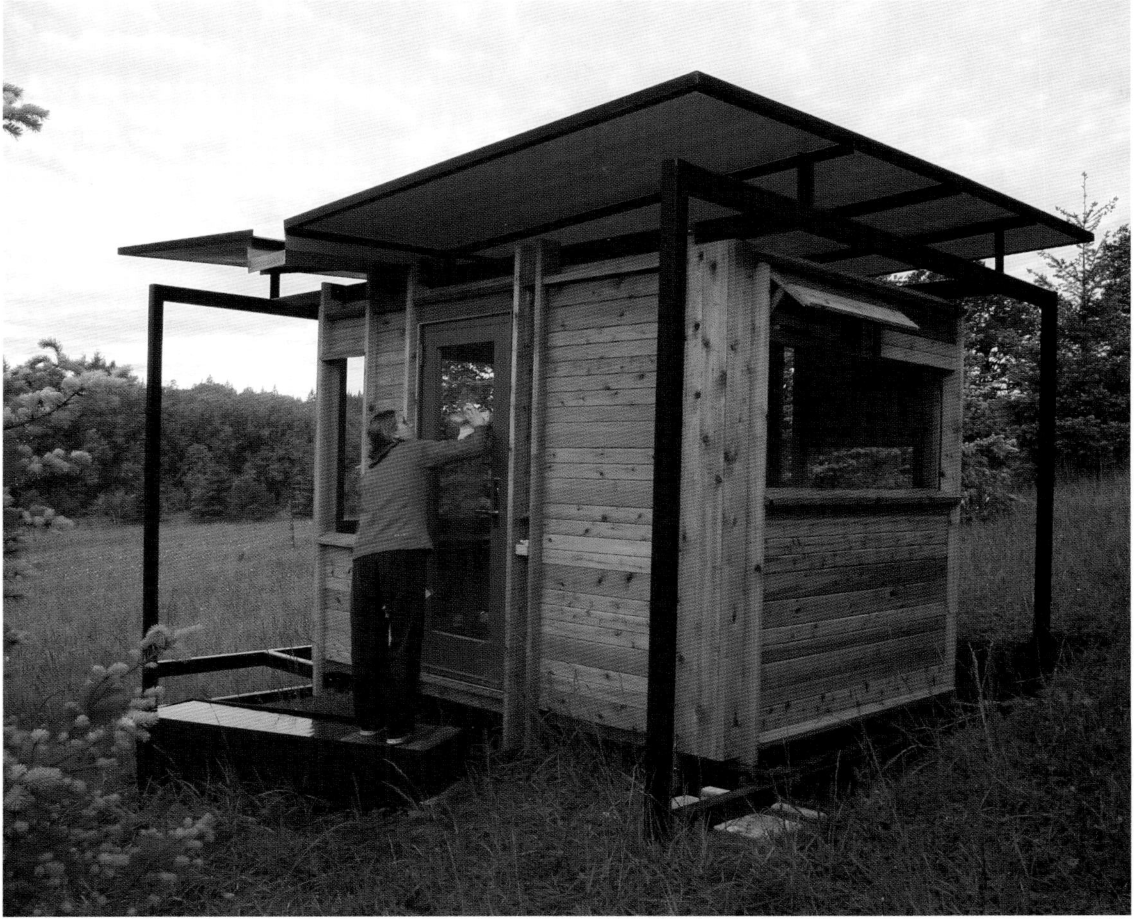

"Our houses are such unwieldy property that we are often imprisoned rather than housed in them," writes Henry David Thoreau in *Walden*. Taking its title from the 1854 classic, Nils Holger Moormann inverses the understanding of home. There is no inside space, only storage. The designer's Walden is a *Wunderkammer* of everything one needs to live the simple life outdoors.

At roughly 12½ feet high by 3½ feet wide by 21 feet long, the wooden box (larch and painted birch plywood) contains, in lieu of a kitchen, a swinging fire cauldron, firewood, grill utensils, beer glasses, and picnic table. For those growing their own vegetables, Moormann created storage space for tools—individual compartments house the shovel, rake, watering can, and wheelbarrow. True to Thoreau, the designer included bookshelves and a seating area. A ladder tucked in the box's section leads to the upper level, where a narrow cushion is just large enough for sleeping. Although a sliding sunroof shelters the area, the designer suggests leaving it open at night so as not to obscure the view of the stars.

WALDEN

Location varies 2006
Nils Holger Moormann

A shiny, anodized aluminum cube perched on the landscape, the Micro Compact Home (m-ch) more closely resembles a lunar lander than any conventional dwelling. To develop the design, architects Richard Horden, Lydia Haack, and John Höpfner teamed with researchers and designers based in London and at the Technical University in Munich (and collaborated with the Tokyo Institute of Technology). They combined technologies gleaned from high-efficiency spaces: aircrafts, yachts, automobiles, and concepts from Japanese teahouses all make appearances in the design. Weighing in at 2.2 tons, the result is essentialist.

Just 105 inches on each side, the m-ch contains everything needed for daily living. The interior is outfitted with two compact double beds, a dining table that seats five, shower and water closet, a well-equipped kitchen, two flat-screen televisions, storage, and Internet and phone connections. The m-ch is sturdy enough to be shipped by truck or airlifted by helicopter into remote areas. It is constructed out of a timber frame structure clad in anodized aluminum panels and insulated with polyurethane. Off the grid, the home can be fitted with a solar cell and turbine energy sources. The design team also considered the long-term impact of the home on the environment; all cladding and connections are recyclable.

MICRO COMPACT HOME

Location varies 2001

Horden Cherry Lee Architects

Haack + Höpfner Architeckten

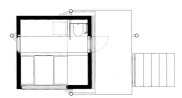

The Little Houses were constructed as a yearlong collective project among students at Parsons The New School for Design, the St. Etienne School of Art and Design in France, and Konstfack University College of Arts, Crafts, and Design in Stockholm. The moveable dwellings imaginatively reuse the existing infrastructure—they ride the rails of a former industrial railway bridge spanning the Black River. With nod to the town's heritage, the *friggebod*, a traditional Swedish cabin, inspired the design.

Seasonal and sustainable, the structures are built from local materials (hardwood, plywood, and acrylic panels—both clear and translucent) and are designed as temporary housing for artists-in-residence from the regional design museum and research center, Formens Hus. The living and sleeping units are equipped with built-in and modular furnishings. The students considered every detail—CNC-routed, decorative plywood cleats hold lighting or serve as clothes hangers. A utilitarian third structure, a service station designed by Parsons faculty member Robert Kirkbride, houses the kitchen and bathroom facilities. Responding to the natural environment, in the summer the compartments can be reconfigured to create a range of outdoor spaces between the cabins. In the winter, the Little Houses slide together and dock at the service station.

LITTLE HOUSES ON THE BLACK RIVER

HÄLLEFORS, SWEDEN 2006

Parsons The New School for Design, New York

Konstfack University College of Arts, Crafts and Design, Sweden

Etienne School of Art and Design, France

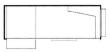

Cologne-based graphic designer Marcell Krings and cabinetmaker Sebastian Mühlhäuser designed Casulo, a concept for living that's both compact and mobile. Their design eases the demands, both physical and ecological, of moving from one apartment to another in a busy metropolis. A complete set of furniture, Casulo assembles in less than ten minutes and ships easily. Unassembled, it fits in the trunk of a Renault Kangoo.

Ready for apartment living, each Casulo unit includes a wardrobe, large desk/table, desk cabinet with locking drawers, an adjustable desk chair, two stools, a single bed and mattress, and a tall set of shelves. The stools and the drawers of the desk cabinet double as storage containers. For transport, the steel frame of the desk/table serves as the structural framework of the Casulo and the frame of the bed is the same size as a four-way European pallet. Constructed out of durable, long-lasting materials, the Casulo keeps trash out of the waste stream. People who move frequently—students, nurses, consultants—no longer have to acquire sets of essentially disposable, inexpensive furnishings whose transportation costs and impact on the environment are higher than the value of the furniture.

CASULO

Location varies 2007

Marcel Krings and Sebastian Mühlhäuser

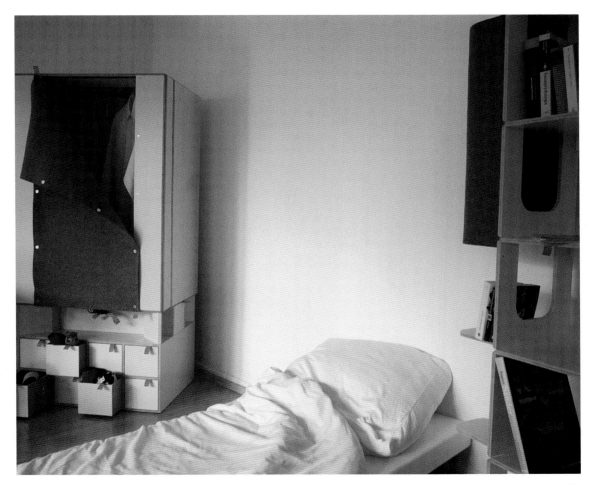

ARCHITECTS

Alchemy Architects
St. Paul, Minnesota
www.weehouses.com

Altius Architecture
Toronto, Canada
www.altius.net

Atelier Tekuto
Tokyo, Japan
www.tekuto.com

BAK Arquitectos
Buenos Aires, Argentina
www.bakarquitectos.com.ar

Bauart Architekten
www.bauart.ch
Zurich, Switzerland

BaumRaum
Bremen, Germany
www.baumraum.de

BILD Design
New Orleans, Louisiana
www.bildit.com

BlueSky Mod
Toronto, Canada
www.blueskymod.com

Boyarsky Murphy
London, United Kingdom
www.boyarskymurphy.com

Casulo
Cologne, Germany
www.mein-casulo.de

Counson Architectes
Vielsalm, Belgium
www.counson-architecte.net

**Float architectural research
and design**
Tucson, Arizona
http://floatarch.com

Flores & Prats Arquitectes
Barcelona, Spain
www.floresprats.com

FNP Architekten
Stuttgart, Germany
www.fischer-naumann.de

Haack + Höpfner. Architekten
Munich, Germany
www.haackhoepfner.de

Horden Cherry Lee Architects
London, United Kingdom
www.hcla.co.uk

Ivan Kroupa Architects
Prague, Czech Republic
www.ivankroupa.cz

Konstfack University
Stockholm, Sweden
www.konstfack.se

Korteknie Stuhlmacher Architecten
Rotterdam, Netherlands
www.kortekniestuhlmacher.nl

Michael Jantzen
Los Angeles, California
www.humanshelter.org

Micro Compact Home
London, United Kingdom
www.microcompacthome.com

Neeson Murcutt Architects
Sydney, Australia
www.neesonmurcutt.com

Nils Holger Moormann
Aschau im Chiemgau, Germany
www.moormann.de

Nomadhome Trading GmbH
Salzburg, Austria
www.nomadhome.com

noroof Architects
Brooklyn, New York
www.noroof.net

Olson Sundberg Kundig Allen Architects
Seattle, Washington
www.oskaarchitects.com

Parsons School of Design
productdesign.parsons.edu

Recetas Urbanas
Seville, Spain
www.recetasurbanas.net

Robbrecht en Daem Architechten
Ghent, Belgium
www.robbrechtendaem.com

Ronan and Erwan Bouroullec
Paris, France
www.bouroullec.com

Sami Rintala
Trondheim, Norway
www.samirintala.com

Saunders Architecture
Bergen, Norway
www.saunders.no

Scape Architects
London, United Kingdom
www.scape-architects.com

sculp(IT)
Antwerp, Belgium
users.telenet.be/sculpit

St. Etienne School of Art and Design
Saint-Etienne, France
www.esadse.fr

Steven Holl Architects
New York City, New York
www.stevenholl.com

Sustain Design Studio Altius Architecture
Toronto, Canada
http://sustain.ca/

Tezuka Architects
Tokyo, Japan
www.tezuka-arch.com

Travis Price Architects
Washington, DC
www.travispricearchitects.com

Tumbleweed Tiny House Company
Sebastopol, California
www.tumbleweedhouses.com

Uni Architects
Cambridge, Massachusetts
www.uni-a.com

Zero Plus architects
Seattle, Washington
http://0-plus.com

This book would not have been possible without the assistance and insight of Ruth Keffer, the design vision of over,under's Chris Grimley and Kelly Smith, and Dung Ngo's editorial guidance. Thank you. **MZ**